Financial Crisis, Populism, and the Path to Prosperity in Latin America

Carroll Ríos de Rodríguez

ACTON INSTITUTE

Christian Social Thought Series
Number 17 • Edited by Kevin Schmiesing

Christian Social Thought Series, Number 17

The Acton Institute acknowledges with gratitude the John Templeton Foundation for its support in the publication of this book.

Cover image: Railway Chihuahua, Mexico
Source: www.istockphoto.com. 01-08-08 © Geoffrey Fritsch

ISSN 10: 1-880595-37-0
ISSN 13: 978-1-880595-37-4

ACTONINSTITUTE
161 Ottawa Avenue, NW, Suite 301
Grand Rapids, Michigan 49503
Phone: 616.454.3080
Fax: 616.454.9454
www.acton.org

Printed in the United States of America

Contents

Foreword

During his visit to Brazil in 2007, Pope Benedict XVI called Latin America the "continent of hope." Similarly, economists, sociologists, and others have frequently noted the entrepreneurial flair of the people of Latin America, pointing to their innovative ways of meeting their needs and those of others in the face of obstacles and hardship.

These descriptions are ambivalent. They envision a bright future but also imply that much potential has thus far been unrealized. Many nations of Central and South America have enjoyed occasional periods of growth and prosperity, yet sustained economic progress adequate to solve the problem of poverty in the region has been elusive.

How to unlock the potential inherent in the creative and talented people of developing nations is a question that has been debated for decades. Pope Paul VI focused the Catholic Church's attention on the problem of drastic international inequalities of wealth in 1967 when he published *Populorum Progressio*. Since then, the world community has learned from experience that a simplistic model of direct aid from governments of rich nations to governments of poor nations is woefully inadequate. Drawing on the experience of intervening years as well as the timeless wisdom of Christian doctrine, Pope Benedict XVI reiterated Paul VI's call for attention to the world's poor in his encyclical of 2009, *Caritas in Veritate*.

As Benedict suggests, the obligations of wealthy nations to do what is in their power to assist the development of poor nations remains. Even more, the obligation of individual Christians who are relatively well off to assist those who are less fortunate must be proclaimed and embraced.

Yet, Benedict also stresses emphatically the responsibilities of governments and citizens within developing nations. In large measure, they are the actors whose decisions will determine whether the economic potential of developing nations will be realized—and, more importantly, whether their own potential as human beings, capable of expressing love of God and neighbor through meaningful work, will be fulfilled.

This focus on the capacity of Latin Americans themselves for bringing about the transformation of their lives inspires this book. Professor Carroll Ríos de Rodríguez combines economic expertise with deep understanding of the region's history, culture, and politics. She demonstrates that the social teaching of the Church, with its focus on the human person, aligns with the findings of development economics concerning the necessity of sound and vibrant institutions such as the family, property rights, and rule of law. These institutions provide the environment within which individual initiative and creativity may freely operate.

If such wisdom, rather than the destructive politics of class conflict, wins the day throughout Latin America, then the likelihood increases that hope and promise will come to fruition in sustained prosperity and human flourishing.

Kevin Schmiesing
Acton Institute

1 Introduction

> For a long time it was thought that poor peoples should remain at a fixed stage of development, and should be content to receive assistance from the philanthropy of developed peoples.... Today the material resources available for rescuing these peoples from poverty are potentially greater than before.... The worldwide diffusion of forms of prosperity should not therefore be held up by projects that are self-centered, protectionist or at the service of private interests. Indeed the involvement of emerging or developing countries allows us to manage the crisis better today.
>
> Pope Benedict XVI, *Caritas in Veritate*, no. 42

Did the world financial crisis that erupted in 2008 affect the poor in Latin America? The short answer is yes. Most economies in Latin America are highly interdependent with European and United States markets through commercial ties. The five years leading up to the economic quake had been good to Latin America, and now the region is struggling to regain momentum. However, economic crises have hit before.

The question we should be asking is: Are there other more meaningful explanations for the region's stubborn poverty rates? During the past several decades, economists have, through historical, empirical, and theoretical studies, identified the institutions that foster economic growth. By institutions, we mean the formal and informal norms, rules, and customs of social order.[1] A house built on rock, on stable, growth-oriented institutions, is better able to withstand the onslaught of a hurricane than a house built on sand (Matt. 7:24–25). This book attempts to show that many countries in Latin America have failed to grow significantly because the institutions of entrepreneurship, the formation of human capital, property rights, and rule of law remain weak.[2] The topsy-turvy road to development owes its winding curves more to these domestic institutional failures than to outside factors such as the recent financial and economic crises.

Institutions frame the activities of interdependent people. Some institutional arrangements work better than others in fostering economic growth and prosperity. An effective institutional architecture can be put in place, such that it is possible for societies to transit from development-resistant rules to rules that encourage wealth creation. Rapid growth in Asia has proven this to be true. This is not the position of an arrogant social engineer who holds out an inflexible blueprint for growth. There is no one-size-fits-all recipe for escaping poverty and achieving development. What is more, top-down reforms, such as changes in legislation, must be respectful of bottom-up customs and conventions that have evolved within each culture over time.[3] Some authors use the term *institutional eco-system* to convey the complexity and changing nature of institutions.

The findings of social scientists on these points coincide with the teaching of the Catholic Church on social and economic

---

1 This is in line with new institutional economics as developed by Douglass North, Ronald Coase, and Oliver Williamson, to name a few.

2 Other important institutions highlighted by the literature include monetary, fiscal, and financial policies.

3 For more on economic and political institutions, see Karol Bodreaux and Paul Dragos Aligica, *Paths to Property: Approaches to Institutional Change in International Development* (London: Institute of Economic Affairs, 2007).

matters. Catholic social teaching (CST) offers guidance as to how economic development may proceed in a manner that is consistent with the dignity of each and every human being. For example, the Church reminds us that institutions are created for and should be conducted with a view toward the good of individual persons. "Individual men," wrote Pope John XXIII, "are necessarily the foundation, cause, and end of all social institutions" (MM, no. 219).[4]

The Church also warns against a top-down organization of society by vigorously defending the principle of subsidiarity. "A community of a higher order," John Paul wrote, "should not interfere in the internal life of a community of a lower order, depriving the latter of its functions, but rather should support it in case of need and help to coordinate its activity with the activities of the rest of society, always with a view to the common good" (CA, no. 48). Higher order institutions such as government have an indispensable role to play, but that role is one of support and coordination; governments must be careful not to replace and thereby damage or destroy the legitimate roles played by lower order institutions such as families, businesses, civic groups, and churches.

In this way, the Church recognizes that true development cannot occur by dictate. Individuals must participate in their own progress out of poverty. "Everyone has the right of economic initiative; everyone should make legitimate use of his talents to contribute to the abundance that will benefit all and to harvest the just fruits of his labor" (CCC, no. 2429).

Entrepreneurship and human capital relate to the person and pertain to the realm of voluntary exchange or markets. Each member of society is first a member of a family. Family structure is relevant to the formation of human capital, which in turn determines how well a player will fare in the productive realm. The Church is committed to the "integral development of man," of

4 A list of Church documents and their abbreviations appears at the end of this text.

a rational, transcendent, free, and responsible human being who should not be obliterated by society. Social institutions must permit each person to fulfill his freely assumed vocation for progress (CV, nos. 17–18). Pope Benedict XVI writes, "the *primary capital to be safeguarded and valued is man, the human person in his or her integrity*: 'Man is the source, the focus and the aim of all economic and social life'" (CV, no. 25, citing GS, no. 62).

Rule of law and property rights are like bridges straddling the realm of voluntary exchange and the realm of government. The concept of rule of law is hard to define. Rule of law essentially serves as an unbiased guarantor of basic human rights and involves an independent and impartial judiciary. This is the kind of just authority endorsed by the *Catechism of the Catholic Church*. Authority, it states, "must not behave in a despotic manner, but must act for the common good as a 'moral force based on freedom and a sense of responsibility'" (CCC, no. 1902, citing GS, no. 74).

One basic human right that should be upheld by the legal system and the courts is the right to property. Secure rights to property are necessary for growth. Because we cannot dispose of that which we do not own, all economic activity is made possible through clearly defined rights. The Church has consistently defended the integrity of private property in the strongest terms. "To own goods privately," Leo XIII wrote in 1891, "is a natural right to man, and to exercise this right ... is not only lawful but clearly necessary" (RN, no. 22). The Church also insists, however, that property ownership carries an obligation to use such property not merely for individual benefit but for the common good. "The goods of this world are originally meant for all," John Paul reminds us; "The right to private property is valid and necessary, but it does not nullify the value of this principle" (SRS, no. 42). Through wise and generous employment of property for both productive and charitable purposes, private property becomes the foundation for escaping poverty and advancing toward prosperity.

The world financial crisis has lent credibility to a public-policy agenda that leads countries away from, instead of toward, the establishment of a solid rule of law, the protection of property rights, the formation of human capital, and the promotion of entrepreneurship. Public opinion has been repeatedly exposed to the notion that the financial crisis is the direct result of unbridled market competition, immoral greed, and excessive liberalization and deregulation. The antidote generally recommended is more government intervention.

Dissenting voices point out that prior to their collapse, financial markets were, indeed, regulated markets. The collapse of financial institutions came on the heels of the bursting of the "housing bubble," initially spurred by a government policy geared at expanding home ownership, a policy favored by both Republican and Democrat politicians. The Federal National Mortgage Association and the Federal Home Loan Mortgage Corporations, usually referred to as Fannie Mae and Freddie Mac, are themselves "government sponsored enterprises" that pushed for lax lending requisites, tax breaks, and more. Regulation is also linked with the "too big to fail" mentality; that is, the notion that government must rescue big players from bankruptcy. Economist Antony Mueller put it this way: "Since Alan Greenspan took office, financial markets in the United States have operated under a quasi-official charter, which says that the central bank will protect its major actors from the risk of bankruptcy."[5] It is thus more accurate to speak of a botchy, contradictory or counterproductive regulatory framework, instead of a nonexistent one. As CST suggests, not all regulation has desirable social and economic effects. While it is true that effective and well-enforced regulation may have prevented certain excesses that contributed to the financial crisis, it is misleading

---

[5] Antony Mueller, "Mr. Bailout," Mises.org, September 30, 2004; Antony P. Mueller, "Financial Cycles, Business Activity, and the Stock Market," *Quarterly Journal of Austrian Economics* 4 (Spring 2001). As cited by Thomas E. Woods Jr. in *Meltdown* (Washington, D.C.: Regnery, 2009), 31–32.

to suggest that simply increasing regulation will prevent such problems in the future.

The erroneous belief that government was somehow absent from the scene before the crisis and that a more intrusive government will prevent future crises, meets up with a resurgence of populism in the Latin American region. Populist leaders who posit the solution to economic crisis in the expanding grasp of government ignore the warning of Pope Benedict: "We do not need a State which regulates and controls everything, but a State which, in accordance with the principle of subsidiarity, generously acknowledges and supports initiatives arising from the different social forces and combines spontaneity with closeness to those in need" (DCE, no. 28). Economic evidence supports the Church's balanced appreciation of the important and irreplaceable roles played by various institutions: family, property, business, and rule of law. The future economic prospects of Latin America depend on fostering these institutions and avoiding the superficially attractive but ultimately destructive solution of populist politics.

To substantiate these claims this book is divided into four chapters. First, it briefly describes the effects of the world financial crisis on Latin America. Second, it analyzes regional trends in poverty during the past decades through the lens of the institutional economics approach. Third, it assesses recent attempts by Latin American governments to address the financial crisis. Finally, it warns against continuing down the road taken by populist political movements. The path to prosperity passes not through centralized political control of economic life but through individual initiative conducted within the context of a just political system and a healthy civil society.

II The Financial Crisis of 2008: Latin America

Realization of the magnitude of the financial crisis that originated in the United States hit the world in September 2008. In February, a somber President George Bush had signed the Economic Stimulus Act. By September, however, the banking and financial world was obviously in turmoil: AIG, Citigroup, Wachovia, Lehman Brothers, and Merrill Lynch, among other well-known firms, were making the headlines.[1] In October, the House of Representatives approved a U.S. $700 billion bailout package for the financial sector.[2] To outside observers, this government move signaled a colossal problem; the sum seemed staggering. Few could anticipate then that by the end of November the total cost of funds dedicated to the bailout would surpass the U.S. $8.5 trillion mark.[3] The U.S. government and the U.S.

---

[1] Interesting sites that trace the financial crisis timeline include: http://timeline.stlouisfed.org/index.cfm?p=timeline and http://www.ny.frb.org/research/global_economy/Crisis_Timeline.pdf.

[2] This bailout package is formally named Troubled Asset Relief Program (TARP), and it allows the U.S. government to purchase assets and equity from financial institutions to strengthen its financial sector.

[3] This is according to some estimates. Paul Joseph Watson, "Cost of Bailout Hits $8.5 Trillion-Total Sum Represents 60 Per Cent of GDP," posted by http://www.propagandamatrix.com/articles/november2008/112608_bailout_cost.htm on November 26, 2008, and cited in *Investment Watch*, http://investmentwatchblog.com/tag/rog/.

Federal Reserve ended up committing $13.9 trillion, although only half of that amount had been spent by June 2009.[4] At any rate, this pledge is more than twice the estimated 2010 GDP for all of Latin America![5]

Experts have described the rollercoaster ride as a financial crisis turned economic crisis turned recession. The recession officially ended in July of 2009 when markets rebounded slightly.[6] More time must pass before observers can calculate a dispassionate estimate of how much damage was done. Speaking at the Japan Society in 2009, the CEO of private equity company Blackstone, Stephen Schwarzman, ventured a ballpark figure: "Between 40 and 45 percent of the world's wealth has been destroyed in little less than a year and a half. This is absolutely unprecedented in our lifetime."[7]

Three observations are in order. First, the turmoil is global in its effects but not all countries tumbled into crisis or continue to be in crisis, nor are those affected going through mirror processes. Second, some of the nations in trouble will recover more speedily than others. Third, no one clearly knows whether more trouble lies ahead; for instance, insistence in Europe on prolonging costly welfare programs in the face of major government deficits may lead to greater upheaval.

---

4 FDIC Supervisory Insights Summer 2009, "Government Support for Financial Assets and Liabilities Announced in 2008 and Soon Thereafter ($ in billions)," http://www.fdic.gov/regulations/examinations/supervisory/insights/sisum09/si_sum09.pdf.

5 According to United Nations Development Fund estimates.

6 As described by Miguel Gutierrez, director of Central American Business Intelligence (CABI), conference presentation, "Perspectivas Económicas 2010 para Guatemala y el Mundo, ¿Fin de la Crisis o Espejismos?," Social and Economic Research Center (CEES), Guatemala, November 17, 2009, http://www.cees.org.gt.

7 Megan Davies and Walden Siew, "45 Percent of the World's Wealth Destroyed: Blackstone CEO," *Reuters*, March 10, 2009, http://www.reuters.com/article/2009/03/10/us-blackstone-idUSTRE52966Z20090310.

In Latin America and elsewhere, people pondered the causes that triggered the crisis.[8] Those who point the finger at politicians and economists caught off guard by the debacle emphasize the "obligation" of leaders and experts to foresee such events and plan accordingly. In fact, the Queen of England posed this very question to the brightest minds in the British Academy. They debated amongst themselves and answered the following: "Your Majesty, the failure to foresee the timing, extent and severity of the crisis and to head it off, while it had many causes, was principally a failure of the collective imagination of many bright people, both in this country and internationally, to understand the risks to the system as a whole."[9]

Queen Elizabeth's question presupposes that, had the British authorities possessed adequate information, they might have acted to avert or to soften the blow. This position begs many other questions: Can governments really accomplish more efficient results than markets, during either a boom or a bust? Or, alternatively, can they do away with economic cycles? What does history teach us? Moreover, were governments, especially the United States government, passive spectators during the making of the crisis, or did their policies and regulations play a role in the financial debacle?

These questions provoke an engaging debate that should enlighten both the social sciences and the realm of public policy. Latin Americans should partake in the discussion, not least because

---

8 For an Austrian economics perspective, see Woods, *Meltdown*. Other interesting analyses of the crisis are afforded by Harry Dent (http://www.hsdent.com) and Peter Schiff (http://www.moneyweek.com/news-and-charts/peter-schiff-free-marketeer-who-predicted-the-crisis-45136.aspx). Both Dent and Schiff predicted the crisis. Some argue that the crisis was not financial in its inception.

9 Letter sent by the British Academy to Her Majesty The Queen, dated July 22, 2009, http://austrianeconomists.typepad.com/files/3e3b6ca8-7a08-11de-b86f-00144feabdc0-1.pdf.

some of our governments are mimicking the actions of their counterparts in the United States and Europe, designing their own stimulus packages and promising more regulation and protectionist policies. These reactions may be antlike in comparison with the mammoth U.S. response, but they still impose costs on the region's inhabitants.

The Economic Situation in Latin America

Following the 2001 to 2002 world recession, Latin America experienced several consecutive years of economic growth. The average annual GDP growth rate between 2003 and 2008 was 4.83 percent; large markets such as Argentina and Peru grew up to 8 percent a year.[10]

Table 1
GDP Growth Rates (1999–2009)

Year	World	United States	Latin America
1999	2.95	3.86	0.2
2000	4.41	4.25	4.0
2001	1.51	0.75	0.4
2002	1.76	1.59	-0.4
2003	2.63	2.70	2.2
2004	4.11	4.21	6.1
2005	3.65	3.52	4.9
2006	3.9	3.5	5.8
2007	3.5	3.2	5.8
2008	5.2	0.43	4.2
2009	3.1	-3.13	-1.9

Source: Numbers vary slightly depending on source. *GDP Growth Rates by Country and Region 1970–2007.* Latin America data are generated in

[10] Rodrigo Delgado Aguilera, et al., *From Steady Growth to Sudden Crisis: How Latin America and the Caribbean Are Coping with the Global Recession*, International Economics Working Paper: IEP WP 09/01, London, Chatham House (May 2009), http://www.chathamhouse.org.uk/publications/papers/view/-/id/744/.

2009 by the Economic Commission for Latin America and the Caribbean (ECLAC) and the International Monetary Fund (IMF) and cited by Terry L. McCoy and Timothy McLendon in *2009 Latin America Business Environment Report*, University of Florida, October, 2009 (retrieved from docs.google.com). For the United States 2008 and 2009, data taken from Trading Economics, http://www.tradingeconomics.com/Economics/GDP-Growth.aspx?Symbol=USD. For Latin America 2008 and 2009, from IMF as cited in Chatham House International Economics Working Paper, May 2006 (see footnote 16). The 1.5 negative growth figure is similar to an April 2009 Consensus Forecast of -1.4 percent.

Most observers reflect on how well Latin America weathered the contagion of the crisis, noting a lesser impact in comparison to past global shakeups and a speedier recovery by 2010 and 2011.[11] ECLAC estimates 2010 growth rates of 3.1 percent for this region.[12] Two economic activities, remittances and foreign direct investments, serve to illustrate how the Latin America economies were impacted by the downturn in the United States and European economies.

Remittances

Large populations of Latin American immigrants living in the United States and, to a lesser degree, Canada and Europe, habitually send remittances to their families in their homelands. Latin America has become the primary destination of remittances, both globally and in per capita terms, in amounts reaching an estimated U.S. $52 billion in 2006 and U.S. $60 billion in 2007,[13] which is

---

[11] OECD Development Center, "Latin America Economic Outlook 2011: How Middle-Class Is Latin America?" OECD 2010, http://www.latameconomy.org/fileadmin/uploads/laeo/Documents/E-book_LEo2011-EN_entier.pdf.

[12] Cited in Terry L. McCoy and Timothy McLendon in *2009 Latin America Business Environment Report*, University of Florida, October 2009 (retrieved from docs.google.com).

[13] The Inter-American Development Bank says the total for 2007 was US $66.5 billion. "Remittances to Latin America and the Caribbean Slower, IADB Fund Says," March 11, 2008, http://www.iadb.org/news/detail.cfm?language=EN&artid=4459&id=4459.

more than the transfers received by the region in international aid and roughly analogous to the volume of direct investment.[14] The precrisis growth in remittances is not necessarily good news for Latin America because it reveals that the region is incapable of generating wealth domestically.

Migrants tend to be young male workers with limited education. Many enter the United States illegally.[15] A high percentage of them are or were employed in the agricultural section or in the construction sector and related fields, which were heavily hit by the housing and financial crisis.[16] According to a Gallup survey conducted in March of 2009, nearly half of all Latino immigrants who have lived in the United States for nineteen years or less send remittances to their families in their home country. The percentage drops for immigrants who have been in the United States for twenty years or more (31 percent) and drops again for U.S.-born Latinos (20 percent). Interestingly, the steadiness of the commitment of these migrants to their families is influenced positively by religious belief and practice.[17]

Measuring total dollars received, Mexico and Brazil are the largest beneficiaries of remittances, but, in terms of percentage of economic activity, these two countries are not as dependent on remittances as their smaller neighbors.[18] A drop in remittances

---

[14] Pablo Fajnzylber and Humberto López, "El impacto de las remesas en el desarrollo de América Latina," first chapter of a World Bank document on remittances and development. http://www.remesasydesarrollo.org/estadisticas/remittances-and-development-lessons-from-latin-america/.

[15] The estimated illegal population in the United States is between 7 and 20 million, mostly from Mexico.

[16] An amount that is still considerably higher than the expected income for the same person in his country of origin.

[17] Gerber Torres, et al., "Half of New Latino Immigrants to U.S. Send Money Abroad," *Gallup*, September 22, 2009, http://www.gallup.com/poll/123140/half-new-latino-immigrants-send-money-abroad.aspx.

[18] James Painter, "US Woes Slow Migrant Remittances," *BBC News*, March 12, 2008, http://news.bbc.co.uk/2/hi/americas/7292216.stm.

is the most significant and lasting blow dealt by the world crisis to Central America.[19]

Table 2
Top Remittance Recipients in Latin America (2007)

Country	Amount (U.S. $)	% GDP
Guyana	$424 million	43%
Haiti	$1.8 billion	35%
Honduras	$2.5 billion	25%
El Salvador	$3.6 billion	18%
Jamaica	$1.9 billion	18%
Mexico	$23.9 billion	2–3%

Source: original data by Inter-American Development Bank (IADB) as presented by James Painter, BBC News (see footnote 23).

In 2010, the Inter-American Development Bank predicted a stabilization of remittance inflows into the region, following a 15 percent drop in 2009.[20] According to the IADB, this was the first decline in remittances since they began measuring annual flows in 2000. This means a comparable decline in the incomes of small rural households.

Interviewed workers confirmed that they were sending less money home during 2008 and 2009 because they had fewer employment opportunities in the United States; a portion of them were cutting into their savings. Some interviewees say their

[19] Jorge Suárez Vélez, "Crisis Financiera en el Mundo y su Efecto para Latino-américa," XII Conference on Financial Supervision sponsored by the Banks Superintendence (SIB) in Guatemala, August 27, 2009.

[20] "Remesas a América Latina caerán 11% en 2009: BID," *Dinero.com*, August 12, 2009, http://www.dinero.com/inversionistas/monedas/remesas-america-latina-caeran-11-2009-bid_62337.aspx. "Remittances to Latin America stabilize after a 15% drop last year—MIF," IDB website, March 4, 2010, http://www.iadb.org/en/news/news-releases/2010-03-04/remittances-to-latin-america-stabilizing-after-15-drop-last-year-mif,6671.html.

families are worse off, while others say that even though they are sending less money home, the purchasing power of the dollar has increased in their respective countries.[21]

Foreign Direct Investment

Foreign Direct Investment (FDI) became a buzzword in the 1980s and 1990s because it promised capital investment for economic growth. Inflows of FDI to Latin America and the Caribbean seemed to pick up around 2005. According to a study conducted by the United Nations Conference on Trade and Development (UNCTAD), the largest recipients of investment were Mexico and Brazil with 27 percent and 25 percent of 2005's total, respectively.[22]

Overall, the financial crisis has significantly affected multinational corporations' investment and growth plans, which are in many cases being postponed, restructured, or cancelled. Masataka Fujita, Chief of UNCTAD's Investment Trends and Data Section, says that FDI inflows declined by 15 percent worldwide in 2008, and that this negative trend was observable in some countries toward the end of 2007. Interestingly, Latin America and the Caribbean did not see FDI inflows diminish in 2007 and 2008;

---

[21] Cesar Muñoz Acebes, "Recession Forces Immigrants to Send Less Cash Home to Families," *Latin American Herald Tribune* (no date), http://www.laht.com/article.asp?ArticleId=335501&CategoryId=12394. Muñoz says the pace of deportations of undocumented workers during the past five years has risen 50 percent.

[22] The entire study can be found in electronic format at http://www.unctad.org/Templates/WebFlyer.asp?intItemID=3489&lang=1. UNCTAD's *World Investment Report 2005: Transnational Corporations and the Internationalization of R&D.* This trend is confirmed by the Economic Commission on Latin America and the Caribbean (ECLAC) Executive Director, Alicia Bárcena, "Latin America and the Caribbean: Challenges and Opportunities in a Time of Crisis," September 11, 2009, http://www.wilsoncenter.org/events/docs/Barcena%20Presentation.ppt.

instead, they increased by 9.4 percent, from $127.3 to $139.3 billion.[23]

However, the international debacle caught up with this region soon thereafter. Foreign Direct Investment to the developing world dropped in 2009 in general terms. In Latin America and the Caribbean, this investment declined by $76.68 billion, which amounts to a drop of 42 percent in comparison to the 2008 mark.[24]

---

23 Masataka Fujita, "Implications of the Financial and Economic Crisis on FDI: An Updated Assessment," Investment Trends and Data Section, *UNCTAD*, April 17, 2009, http://nku.com.cn/UploadFile/200941402013964.pdf.

24 "Foreign Direct Investment in Latin America and the Caribbean," ECLA Briefing Paper, May 2010, http://www.eclac.org/cgi-bin/getProd.asp?xml=/publicaciones/xml/2/39422/P39422.xml&xsl=/ddpe/tpl-i/p9f.xsl&base=/prensa/tpl-i/top-bottom.xsl.

III The Crisis and Poverty in Latin America

Latin America appears to be less vulnerable today than it has been in the past, when international economic difficulties wreaked havoc on the region's finances. The 1981–1982 recession, for example, led to a widespread debt crisis in Latin America, causing economic stagnation, inflation, and unemployment. Similarly, the "Tequila crisis" of 1994–1995 (when Mexico devalued the peso) and the Russian financial crisis of 1998 both resulted in serious economic damage throughout Latin America. This improved stability, the experts say, must be due in part to the implementation of sounder macro-economic policies.[1] This time around, few countries greeted the crisis with high inflation rates, overvalued currencies, or huge fiscal deficits.

Yet, the wisdom of the contemporary responses of some Latin American governments may be questioned. Some governments announced stimulus packages to combat the effects of the crisis.[2] Combating poverty is a leading justification for these programs. One of many examples is the forum titled "Fiscal Policy in Times of Crisis: Volatility, Social Cohesion and the Political Economy

1 See, for instance, *The Global Financial and Economic Storm: How Bad Is the Weather in Latin America and the Caribbean?* World Bank, Latin America and the Caribbean Region, April 22, 2009.

2 The stimulus programs are part of anticyclical fiscal and monetary policies that seek to avoid high unemployment rates, among other things.

of Reform," convened by a host of international and diplomatic organisms, including the Economic Commission for Latin America and the Caribbean (ECLAC) and the European Union. Held in Uruguay in May 2009, the forum sought to guide and unify public policy in Latin America and the Caribbean. The meeting objectives refer to the fight against poverty and the promotion of social cohesion. *Social cohesion* is a phrase that has recently gained popularity in multilateral organisms; it lumps together poverty, inequality and social exclusion.[3] The implication behind Queen Elizabeth's question is present here too because the users of the term firmly believe that state-run programs must tackle these burdens. The meeting documents state: "Fiscal policies face, in Latin America and the Caribbean as well as in Europe, the challenge to stabilize economic growth through stimuli and anti-cyclical measures, but also to proffer instruments that protect the most vulnerable populations from these negative distributive impacts."[4]

In practice, the stimulus plans announced or implemented by the regions' authorities vary widely in content. Peru, for instance, centered on public works such as schools and on attracting more foreign investment for infrastructure. Brazil cut some taxes. Mexico supported medium and small enterprises and undertook housing and antipoverty programs.[5]

---

3 *Social cohesion* is a term adopted officially by European Union and Latin American public servants at the III Summit of the European Union, Latin America and the Caribbean held in Guadalajara, Mexico, in 2004, http://ec.europa.eu/external_relations/la/sc/sc_es/01_what_es.htm.

4 "Fiscal Policy in Times of Crisis: Volatility, Social Cohesion and the Political Economy of Reform," Forum held in Montevideo, Uruguay, May 19–20, 2009. This forum also shows how foreign governments influence policy initiatives in Latin America, often by linking policy reform to aid, http://www.ec.europa.eu/external_relations/lac/fiscalforum/2009_05_prog_es.pdf.

5 Roger F. Noriega, "Latin America and the Economic Crisis: Going It Alone," *Latin American Outlook*, American Enterprise Institute for Public Policy Research (June 2009).

Thus, governments around the world are acting on the premise that the global financial and economic crisis has hurt and will continue to hurt the poor. A corollary assumption is that the government must protect these "vulnerable populations."

Concern for those who cannot meet their own needs is at the heart of Catholic social teaching, and is usually affirmed in Latin America and elsewhere as the *preferential option for the poor*. "This is an option, a special form of primacy in the exercise of Christian charity" Pope John Paul II wrote, "to which the whole tradition of the Church bears witness. It affects the life of each Christian inasmuch as he or she seeks to imitate the life of Christ, but it applies equally to our social responsibilities and hence to our manner of living, and to the logical decisions to be made concerning our ownership and the use of goods" (SRS, no. 42). This principle behooves us to examine carefully the actual impact of the financial crisis on the poor, as well as the effectiveness of government and societal responses intended to assist these populations. What is the best way to address the problem of poverty? To answer the question accurately, we must analyze briefly the nature of poverty.

"The natural state of man is abject poverty," Manuel Ayau reminds us.[6] This assertion should not be taken as an excuse to do nothing but rather as a realistic assessment of the challenges that we face. "*Human misery is a clear sign of man's natural condition of frailty and of his need for salvation*" (CSD, no. 183). In the same way, when Jesus stated "you shall always have the poor among you," he was not discouraging efforts either to measure poverty or to alleviate it, but rather he was highlighting the opportunity for Christians to exercise compassion toward those less fortunate.

The *Compendium of the Social Doctrine* continues in this vein: "Christian realism, while appreciating on the one hand the praiseworthy efforts being made to defeat poverty, is cautious on the other hand regarding ideological positions and Messianistic beliefs

---

[6] Manuel Ayau, "La distribución de la riqueza," in *El proceso económico* (Mexico: Diana, 1995), 3–1.

that sustain the illusion that it is possible to eliminate the problem of poverty completely from this world" (no. 183). This passage cautions against yearning for a utopian future of identical incomes and material equality otherwise defined, least of all when relative differences in income are the result of free and responsible actions on the part of market participants.

What, then, is poverty? Theologian John Bolt writes, "[P]overty is necessarily a relative … term. As one of the Oxford English Dictionary definitions states: Poverty is a 'relative lack of money or material possessions.'"[7] Poverty refers to an absence or lack of something. In the tradition of CST, poverty is not an exclusively material or economic concept: "The denial or the limitation of human rights—as, for example, the right to religious freedom, the right to share in the building of society, the freedom to organize and form unions, or the right to take initiative in economic matters—do these not impoverish the human person as much as, if not more than, the deprivation of material goods?" (SRS, no. 15). This point reminds us that every action or program intended to address poverty must at the same time respect fundamental human rights and the dignity of the person; if it does not, material gains might be offset by losses in other dimensions of human wellbeing, thus failing to effect real progress against poverty in the broader sense of the term.

The concept of poverty is relative in three ways, adds sociologist Carlos Sabino. A person is relatively poorer or richer than another person or group of persons, or as opposed to a past state of affairs or in relation to some reasonable expectation.[8] Relative conditions of poverty change constantly over time. Wealth is not a finite or a fixed amount. In game theory jargon, the economic

---

7 John Bolt, "Christian Obligations: 'The Poor You Will Always Have with You,'" *Journal of Markets & Morality* 7 (Fall 2004): 467–93.

8 Carlos Sabino, "Mitos sobre la pobreza," http://paginas.ufm.edu/sabino/ingles/book/mitos_pobreza.pdf.

realm is not a zero-sum game.[9] This is a critically important point. Although CST tends to emphasize the importance of charity and the just distribution of goods, we must also be cognizant of the ways in which individual actions and public policy may affect the overall potential of the economy to continue to expand the pool of goods and services available to be distributed. Without increasing wealth creation, equitable distribution will be inadequate to meet the needs of a growing world population. The social sciences seek to measure and track poverty trends within countries and globally, and they explore income inequality. An objective standard of absolute poverty is at the root of measurement attempts. Inherent difficulties plague these quantifying schemes, and, of course, estimates vary depending on how each analysis is designed.

All the evidence indicates, however, that Latin America had made dramatic advances in the years leading up to 2009: fewer infants died, water was cleaner, more people were employed, and millions rose above the ranks of poverty and extreme poverty.[10] Progress was not restricted to Latin America. This evidence of dramatic improvements in per capita income around the world bewilders many in the churches, the media, and politics. It is hard to adjust a hardened mindset: We have heard repeated for years that poverty is on the rise.[11]

---

9 See, for instance, Manuel Ayau, *Not a Zero-Sum Game* (Guatemala: Universidad Francisco Marroquín, 2007).

10 Noriega, "Latin America and the Economic Crisis." See also Peter Leeson, "Two Cheers for Capitalism?" http://www.peterleeson.com/Two_Cheers_for_Capitalism.pdf.

11 Examples abound: Rodrigo Lastrero, "La pobreza reina en el mundo hispano," Univisión, September 28, 2005, http://www.univision.com/content/content.jhtml?cid=674281. "El aumento de la pobreza en América Latina, la secuela más ingrata de la crisis," *degerencia.com*, August 27, 2009, http://www.degerencia.com/noticia/29341/el-aumento-de-la-pobreza-en-america-latina-la-secuela-mas-ingrata-de-la-crisis.

Still, Latin America is by no means a uniformly prosperous and thriving region. Columbia University professor Xavier Sala-i-Martin says Latin America has achieved mixed results over the past three decades. The region started on par with Asia in the 1970s. "The fraction of the world's poor that live in Latin America declined from 4.3% in 1970 to 1.7% in 1980. It then increased to 3.7% in 1990 and 4.8% in 2000."[12] Put in global context, the performance of Latin America is disappointing when compared to parts of Asia but encouraging as contrasted to large parts of the African continent, especially the sub-Sahara region.[13]

Social scientists and religious leaders are also concerned with income *inequality*. Even among those who concede gains in wealth creation, there are some who stress a growing inequality of income between rich and poor, or developed and less developed nations. Pope Benedict has reiterated this common theme in CST: "*The world's wealth is growing in absolute terms, but inequalities are on the increase*" (CV, no. 22).

Although there is no consensus on the topic, a long article reviewing the debate, published by *The Economist*, concludes that "the official World Bank data, used by the UN and other agencies, are too pessimistic: poverty has most likely fallen faster than these widely cited figures suggest, and possibly fast enough to reduce the global headcount of those living on less than a dollar a day,

---

[12] Xavier Sala-i-Martin, "Global Inequality Fades as the Global Economy Grows," in *2007 Index of Economic Freedom: The Link Between Economic Opportunity and Prosperity*, ed. Tim Kane, Kim R. Holmes, and Mary Anastasia O'Grady (Washington, D.C.: The Heritage Foundation and *The Wall Street Journal*, 2007).

[13] "More or Less Equal?" *The Economist*, March 11, 2004, http://www.economist.com/node/2498851?story_id=2498851; Victor Montecarlo, "Disminuye Pobreza en el Mundo," *International Business Times*, September 9, 2008, http://www.ibtimes.com.mx.

even as population rises."[14] The magazine goes further: There is no evidence that the expansion in wealth was obtained at the cost of the poor by widening the gap in inequality.

These findings do not necessarily contradict the views expressed in *Caritas*. Benedict's appraisal of economic inequality recognizes the complexity of the measurements pertinent to such a claim. He notes that development has "many overlapping layers," and that the "demarcation line between rich and poor countries" is not clear and bright. In the context of his criticism of inequality, he mentions "new forms of poverty" emerging in "rich countries"; he obviously does not have in mind here a simple imbalance between the incomes of rich and poor. He is concerned, too, with "wasteful" and "consumerist" activity in poorer nations, as the wealthy display their riches ostentatiously while the masses struggle to survive (CV, no. 22).

The pope's diagnosis of the causes of the problem of inequality makes clear that he does not view government transfer programs as a silver bullet. Among the causes he identifies are abuses of human rights sometimes perpetrated by both "large multinational companies" and "local producers"; the diversion of international aid from its intended purpose, the result of irresponsibility on the part of both "the chain of donors" as well as the "beneficiaries"; rich countries' "excessive zeal" for protecting intellectual property; and, within poor nations, harmful "social norms of behavior," which inhibit economic progress (CV, no. 22).

Thus, both CST and economic evidence point to the fact that solutions to poverty must be multifaceted, tailored to individual circumstances and needs, and respectful of human dignity and of the right of individuals to participate in and direct their own development. Nonetheless, the United Nations' Economic Commission for Latin America (ECLAC) continues to advocate the same basic

---

14 "More or Less Equal?"

strategy in place since its founding: government-run and designed regulation of markets and programs for the poor, accompanied by injections of foreign aid.[15] Speaking at an ECLAC conference, Helen Clark, administrator of the U.N. Development Program, concluded: "The market by itself will not eliminate poverty, nor will it deliver equity, nor justice."

Throughout history, people who have been free to enter into voluntary and responsible exchange through open markets do experience rising living standards to an extent that, for many, the severity of poverty is lessened, even if it is not completely eradicated. In developed countries, poor families today have access to goods and services that were not available to royalty centuries ago (chocolate, washing machines, telephones, and so forth). While many economists and CST also caution that markets alone will not ensure equity and justice, they would not go so far as to buy into ECLAC's apparent tendency to downplay the role of markets in producing the resources necessary to ameliorate poverty. Clark and ECLAC's Executive Director, Alicia Bárcena, agree that the current international organization strategy calls for better governments, better markets (achieved by more regulation), and a more active citizenry, in that order.[16]

---

[15] Initial ECLAC policy recommendations revolved around its first president's theories regarding Industrialization through Substitution of Imports (ISI). Raúl Prebisch's protectionist prescriptions were tried in many Latin American countries throughout the 1960s and 1970s but lost popularity in the 1980s. ECLAC came on board the trend to open markets to international trade and the establishment of trade blocks. Bárcena´s discourse seems to backtrack to Prebisch's original faith in governments. See also Agencias EFE y AFP, "Región tendrá 9 millones más de pobres en 2009," *Siglo Veintiuno*, Guatemala, November 20, 2009, 20. See also ECLAC's official site: http://www.eclac.org/cgi-bin/getProd.asp?xml=/prensa/noticias/comunicados/3/37833/P37833.xml&xsl=/prensa/tpl/p6f.xsl&base=/tpl/top-bottom.xsl. ECLAC uses the survey method described above to estimate poverty rates in the region.

[16] Bárcena and Clark are not only worried about the financial crisis. They feel this strategy is necessary to face environmental, food, and energy crises.

This ranking of priorities gets the order exactly wrong. Formation of responsible, productive, and ethical citizens is the foundation of economic progress and integral human development. Markets must be encased in the rule of law but, in many cases, their more efficient and equitable operation requires decreasing (or at least reforming) existing regulations, not the reverse. Governments must indeed get better, but this means cleaning up corruption, streamlining the path to economic opportunity (especially for the poor; for example, by eliminating costly and time-consuming processes that prevent individuals from starting businesses), and ensuring free and democratic governance by maintaining a division of powers and adhering to constitutional and statutory law.

As has already been seen, CST stresses the role of Christian charity and personal responsibility in exercising the preferential option for the poor. The Church has also recognized the structural dimensions of poverty and has called for action at the political level. The popes have consistently argued that developed nations should provide government-to-government aid to low-income nations. Societies and nations are obligated to commit to the development of peoples (SRS, nos. 9, 32).

With that said, papal statements have grown increasingly pointed in their warnings about the dangers of this type of aid and the abuses to which it often gives rise.[17] *Caritas in Veritate* introduces clear warnings regarding redistributive policies from prosperous nations to poorer countries:

> International organizations might question the actual effectiveness of their bureaucratic and administrative machinery, which is often excessively costly. At times it happens that

---

"Se requieren alianzas más eficaces entre Estado y mercado," ECLAC Press Bulletin, November 4, 2009, 7.

[17] For a thorough overview of CST on development aid, see Philip Booth, *International Aid and Integral Human Development* (Grand Rapids: Acton Institute, 2011).

> those who receive aid become subordinate to the aid-givers, and the poor serve to perpetuate expensive bureaucracies which consume an excessively high percentage of funds intended for development. Hence it is to be hoped that all international agencies and non-governmental organizations will commit themselves to complete transparency (see CV, no. 47).

The encyclical cautions against creating perverse incentive structures: "[aid] can sometimes lock people into a state of dependence and even foster situations of localized oppression and exploitation in the receiving country. Economic aid, in order to be true to its purpose, must not pursue secondary objectives" (CV, no. 58). Finally, the pope encourages donors to treat the poor with respect.

Is foreign aid truly the antidote for Latin America's woes? One insight comes from a meeting sponsored by the International Fund for Agricultural Development (IFAD) in April 2009, where attendees discussed the impact of the global financial crisis on eleven Latin American countries: Bolivia, Brazil, Colombia, Dominican Republic, El Salvador, Guatemala, Honduras, Mexico, Nicaragua, Paraguay, and Peru. These countries were selected because more poor people live there than in other countries in the region. The conference hammered out the well-established fact that most of the poor and extremely poor live in rural areas and in many cases are indigenous in origin. More revealing is the observation that "social programs and targeted financial benefit schemes relieve but do not solve the condition of poor people" and that "the amount of public or private transfers has not shown a clear link to poverty reduction."[18] The insight is noteworthy for two reasons. First, it emanates from practical experience. Second, it is likely to

[18] "From Financial Crisis to Rural Social Crisis in Latin America," Summary Report on International Fund for Agricultural Development (IFAD) Conference, Rome, April 23–24, 2009; http://www.ifad.org/media/press/2009/21.htm.

be honest because it is unexpected. One would expect IFAD to be more comfortable with affirming the Bárcena-Clark posture than with confessing to deficient policy results.

The IFAD meeting's realism is confirmed by other studies.[19] William Easterly tracks the results of the "adjustment with growth" plans espoused by the World Bank and the International Monetary Fund (IMF) from around 1980 to 1999. Latin American countries each received an average of five adjustment loans during the 1980s, time during which the per capita growth rate fell drastically. Easterly concludes: "There was much lending, little adjustment, and little growth.... The lending was there but the growth wasn't."[20] He concludes that the Latin American countries that finally did prosper in the 1990s had implemented growth-oriented reforms, in which case growth is attributable to these changes and not to the loans received.

Some policy makers suggest that the deficiencies result from insufficient aid—if only donor nations could give more, more, more! However, people directly involved with international cooperation efforts are converging to the IFAD stance. The World Bank directly attributes the decline in poverty rates to "greater respect for production, consumption, savings and investment decisions of each person," particularly in Asia.[21]

Besides the problems of excessive bureaucracy and aid-dependency pointed out by Pope Benedict XVI, government-to-government aid fosters perverse political incentives. Aid rewards governing elites that perpetuate poverty or that are corrupt or violent. It is also connected with weakening democratic practices. Aid alters economic incentives in markets, whether it is

---

[19] See for instance the Gapminder Graph comparing aid and income to Haiti and Tanzania, http://tinyurl.com/ybphug8.

[20] William Easterly, *The Elusive Quest for Growth: Economists' Adventures and Misadventures in the Tropics* (Cambridge: MIT Press, 2002), 102–3.

[21] Montecarlo, "Disminuye Pobreza en el Mundo."

properly invested or not. It does not necessarily reach the target populations.[22]

Easterly speaks graphically of "governments killing growth" in at least six ways: (1) spawning high inflation, (2) running huge deficits, (3) pushing commercial banks out of the market through regulation or by monopolizing banking services, (4) encouraging black markets and corruption, (5) failing to provide basic services, and (6) shutting down economies. Easterly backtracks to clarify that while government policies can lead to bad growth or no growth at all, governments do not cause growth *per se*.[23]

A more recent crop of economic literature is exploring what the poor are actually doing for themselves. This line of research breeds hope, as it has found that people in the lowest social echelons create wealth even under dire, violent, and unstable conditions; even when forced to work in precarious, informal markets with no legal backing for their basic rights to property, contracts, and more.[24] Because one of the obstacles faced by informal workers is blocked access to commercial bank loans, a host of experiments in microcredit lending surfaced in recent decades. These yield positive results as trustworthy beneficiaries start productive ventures. One of the most famous outfits is the Grameen Bank, set up by Nobel Peace Prize winner Muhammad Yunus. In Bangladesh alone, this self-financing bank has helped 58 percent of the borrowers

---

22 *International Aid and Integral Human Development.*

23 Easterly, *Elusive Quest for Growth*, 217–39.

24 Hernando De Soto and Enrique Ghersi, *El Otro Sendero* (Perú: Editorial El Barranco, 1986). For interesting case studies see Alvaro Vargas Llosa, *Lessons from the Poor: Triumph of the Entrepreneurial Spirit* (Oakland, Calif.: The Independent Institute, 2008); also Benjamin Powell, editor, *Making Poor Nations Rich: Entrepreneurship and the Process of Economic Development* (Stanford: Stanford University Press, 2007). For a synopsis, see "Making Poor Nations Rich," The Independent Institute, http://www.independent.org/publications/books/book_summary.asp?bookID=70.

rise out of poverty. It has obtained similar results in countries of diverse ethnic and religious backgrounds.[25]

Take, for instance, Raymunda Yax from Cantel, Quetzaltenango, in the Guatemalan highlands. With less than $2,000 in capital provided by the Foundation for Financial Assistance to Development and Social Service Institutions (known by its Spanish acronym FAFIDESS), she was able to get back on her feet as a wholesale distributor of fashion jewelry, setting up her own stall in a busy market. She had previously experienced setbacks. When she was selling door to door, her whole stock was stolen off a bus, and at one point her clients owed her a devastating total of $2,500 in credit. Thanks to FAFIDESS, she has time to run her store and design original earrings, and is dreaming of opening a second shop. Members of Rotary Clubs in Guatemala established FAFIDESS in 1986. The entity finances micro and small businesses—mostly headed by women—and also teaches credit recipients basic business and accounting skills.[26]

Another interesting story is that of Dr. John Hatch who, in Bolivia in 1984, started "village banking" by putting low-income farmers in charge of a loan program. Through this methodology, entire communities serve as guarantors for each other's loans, thus enabling members to set up or grow their micro-enterprises. Hatch founded FINCA International in 1985 with the mission of providing "financial services to the world's lowest-income entrepreneurs so they can create jobs, build assets and improve their standard of living." As is the case with similar organizations, most FINCA loans go out to dependable women in Latin

[25] Muhammad Yunus, "How Could the World Change Through Microcredit," Lecture at Universidad Francisco Marroquín, Guatemala, December 10, 2007. http://newmedia.ufm.edu/gsm/index.php?title=How_could_the_world_change_through_microcredit.

[26] Raymunda Yax tells her own story in a short video clip, www.youtube.com/watch?v=JcxZpsW6wag.

America, Asia, and Africa, and they exhibit a positive record for combating poverty.[27]

Microcredit lending does not cure all ills, nor is every beneficiary brilliantly successful. Some nonprofit lending methodologies have proven deficient and a few lenders have been accused of dishonest practices or charging excessively high interest rates. Nonetheless, the evidence suggests that many programs have made significant contributions to advancing the wellbeing of low-income families in Latin America. There are many stories like that of Raymunda Yax. Microfinance programs enable entrepreneurs to pursue self-determined goals and, in many cases, reinforce their skills. According to a study conducted by Norwegian economics professor Oystein Strom, the microcredit and microbanking sector is itself a remarkable story. These types of loans have grown 40 percent worldwide since 2000, and were not affected by the 2008 financial crisis.[28] The lending strategy bets on the resourcefulness, market intuition, and self-reliance of the beneficiaries.

Centuries ago, Adam Smith detected that the tendency to "truck and barter" is natural; in all societies some people are alert to opportunity.[29] Wealth is created, adds economist James Gwartney, when the actions of entrepreneurs lead to the production of goods valued by consumers more highly than their cost. Joshua Hall and Russell Sobel conclude, "Entrepreneurship is the catalyst for economic growth and progress. A primary determinant of

---

27 For more information on John Hatch and FINCA, see http://www.finca.org/site/c.6fIGIXMFJnJ0H/b.6088503/k.4ADB/John_Hatch_and_FINCA.htm.

28 Frida Hessel, "Microfinanzas, una historia de éxito, según experto noruego," *Microdinero, Diario Global de Microfinanzas*, March 18, 2011, http://www.microdinero.com/nota.php?subseccion=D6&notId=3291.

29 James Gwartney, foreword to *Lessons from the Poor*, by Alvaro Vargas Llosa, vii.

entrepreneurship is economic freedom."[30] Unfortunately, not all countries treat entrepreneurship as what it is—a path to growth:

> In many societies, the rules of the game incorporate barriers that restrict entrepreneurial activity and allow political officials to play favorites. This *institutional* structure undermines the operation of markets and encourages people to seek wealth through "legal plunder"—the use of the political process to take from some and give to others, particularly those in political power. When this incentive structure is present, even entrepreneurs will try to get ahead by seeking political favors.[31]

Cuba constitutes a graphic and drastic example. Shortly after the 1959 revolution, the Castro regime consolidated central control and oversight of all investments on the island. The system tended to favor those closest to the regime. Breaking ground with communist ideology, the Raul Castro regime now permits self-employed Cubans, called "cuentapropistas," to devote themselves to one of the 178 activities laid out in law. The activities listed include bookkeeping and cleaning public bathrooms, and the rules are so detailed that they specify how many clients a homespun restaurant ("paladar") can serve at a time, where activities are to be carried out, and when and who can employ nonfamily members. We have yet to see how these small enterprises will fare, as they are also heavily burdened by tax requirements.[32]

Estimating the costs created by obstacles to entrepreneurial activity is difficult, because such an exercise requires imagin-

---

[30] Joshua C. Hall and Rossell S. Sobel, "Freedom, Entrepreneurship, and Economic Growth," *Lessons from the Poor*, by Alvaro Vargas Llosa, 247.

[31] James Gwartney, foreword to *Lessons from the Poor*, by Alvaro Vargas Llosa, viii.

[32] "Comienza la era de los cuentapropistas en Cuba," *La Gaceta*, Argentina, September 25, 2010, http://www.lagaceta.com.ar/nota/400184/mundo/Comienza-era-cuentapropistas-Cuba.html. The article is unsigned.

ing an alternative and nonexistent scenario. Nonetheless, Latin Americans are painfully aware of the costs imposed by such practices as excessive red tape to register or close a business, the arbitrary enforcement of property rights, or the hidden tax burden of hiring private guards because security forces do not perform their duties. Corruption and bribes also impose unquantifiable costs. Some interpret northbound migration as an effect of these hurdles within domestic markets. The *Doing Business 2011* report summarizes the point succinctly:

> Where business regulation is transparent and efficient, opportunities are less likely to be based on personal connections or special privileges, and more economic activity is likely to take place in the formal economy, where it can be subject to beneficial regulations and taxation. Since 2003, when the Doing Business project started, policy makers in more than 75% of the world's economies have made it easier to start a business in the formal sector. A recent study using data collected from company registries in 100 economies over 8 years found that economies with efficient business registration systems have a higher firm entry rate and greater business density on average.[33]

The poor are not helpless victims, but a creative force endowed with entrepreneurial spirit. Yunus says: "People can change their life. It is not government that should change people's lives. Governments create a nurturing environment so that then people can do their thing."[34] Recent studies reaffirm this insight. Peruvian intellectual Alvaro Vargas Llosa edited a book titled, *Lessons from*

---

[33] "Executive Summary," *Doing Business 2011* (Washington, D.C.: The International Bank for Reconstruction and Development/The World Bank, 2010), http://www.doingbusiness.org/~/media/fpdkm/doing%20 business/documents/annual-reports/english/db11-fullreport.pdf.

[34] Yunus, "How Could the World Change Through Microcredit," Lecture at Universidad Francisco Marroquín, Guatemala, December 10, 2007.

the Poor: Triumph of the Entrepreneurial Spirit.[35] It contains five detailed descriptions of "rags to riches" stories; two in Peru, one in Argentina, one in Nigeria, and one in Kenya. Vargas Llosa shows how people with practically no investment capital or formal education can recognize and seize business opportunities. The Añaños family started producing bottled soda in their garage in impoverished Ayacucho, Peru, during the height of the Sendero Luminoso (Shining Path) guerrilla warfare when social conflict caused international brands to cease distribution in their locality. The family initially used recycled beer bottles and no labels. They innovated a low-cost operation that in time proved to be a versatile way of expanding into new markets. The production procedure and distribution system helped them grow into a multinational business operating in other Latin American countries and Thailand.[36]

Another example in Peru is that of Aquilino Flores. He went from washing cars to running a complex, vertically integrated textile and clothing manufacturing company and a chain of department stores in Peru and Venezuela. The Flores family has created employment for over 5,000 people. Annual sales exceed $100 million. The Flores firm Topy Top has become an important exporter ($85 million).[37]

The lesson is one that P. T. Bauer stressed as far back as 1948 when he affirmed that the expansion of the rubber agro-industry in Malaya and Indonesia in the 1930s was proof against the "vicious circle of poverty" because much of the seed capital came from very small local investors and traders. Though mostly uneducated and poor, they had sufficient knowledge and sense to

35 Vargas Llosa, *Lessons from the Poor.*

36 Daniel Córdova, "Amid Hopelessness, Hopeful Investment: The Case of the Añaños Family and Kola Real," *Lessons from the Poor*, 1–53.

37 Daniel Córdova, "Defeating Poverty Doing Business: The Case of the Flores Family and Topy Top," *Lessons from the Poor*, 55–119.

seize an entrepreneurial opportunity for economic betterment.[38] The "vicious circle of poverty," rebaptized as the "poverty trap," continues to persuade some academics. Jeffrey Sachs, for instance, calls for massive transfers to such helpless indigents.[39] Bauer would have challenged Sachs by pointing out that "throughout history innumerable individuals, families, groups, societies, and countries—both in the West and the Third World—have moved from poverty to prosperity without external donations. All developed countries began as underdeveloped."[40] Nations became rich without foreign aid and in the midst of spurts of population growth.[41] Pope Benedict XVI is forceful when he writes: "The poor are not to be considered a 'burden,' but a resource, even from the purely economic point of view" (CV, no. 35). Imagine what the poor could do within a growth-stimulating environment that lends them wings instead of anvils.

---

38 P. T. Bauer, "Remembranzas de estudios pasados: Volviendo sobre los primeros pasos," trans. from English of original, published in *Pioneers in Development*, ed. Gerald M. Meir and Dudley Seers (New York: Oxford University Press 1984), http://www.eumed.net/cursecon/textos/bauer-remembranza.htm.

39 See for instance the World Bank Working Paper No. 5012 by J. Humberto López and Luis Servén, "Too Poor to Grow," August 2009, cited by author López in "Demasiado Pobres Para Poder Crecer," Guatemala: *Siglo Veintiuno*, November 24, 2009.

40 P. T. Bauer, "Disregard of Reality," *The Cato Journal* 7 (Spring/Summer 1987): 31.

41 James A. Dorn, "P. T. Bauer's Liberal Market Vision," *Ideas on Liberty* 50 (October 2000), http://www.thefreemanonline.org/featured/p-t-bauers-market-liberal-vision/.

IV Incentives and Institutions

There is no consensus regarding income convergence (bringing developing nations' per capita incomes into line with those of developed nations), but opinion has coalesced around the fact that institutions matter. The right incentives lead to wealth creation; the wrong incentives lead to wealth destruction. As seen above, entrepreneurship is pivotal. So are property rights, the rule of law, and the formation of human capital within the family.

The consensus of great minds on this point is partly attributable to a plethora of empirical studies. Much can be learned from annual indexes such as *Doing Business*,[1] the Fraser Institute's Economic Freedom of the World Project, Transparency International's Corruption Index, the Heritage Foundation and *The Wall Street Journal*'s Index of Economic Freedom, and the Institutional Quality Index.[2] We will explore the implications of the last two of these indexes.

The *Index of Economic Freedom* measures how free entrepreneurs are in each country, whether or not property rights are upheld, and whether citizens live within a stable political environment

1 Published by the World Bank, *Doing Business* measures the legal and administrative obstacles to setting up and operating a business in 183 countries.

2 There is a new index in the works: A Rule of Law Index, as conceptualized by the World Justice Project, www.worldjusticeproject.org.

framed by the rule of law. The index measures other related factors, such as fiscal and financial policies and the size of government. The overarching conclusion is that "the nations with the most economic freedom are also the most prosperous."[3] Economic freedom is defined as "the fundamental right of every human to control his or her own labor and property. In an economically free society, individuals are free to work, produce, consume, and invest in any way they please, with that freedom both protected by the state and unconstrained by the state."[4]

Furthermore, the index shows that economies can be stimulated merely by the initiation of a liberalization program: Countries that had improved the most as compared with other years were the ones that grew the most. The opposite is also true: Restrictions make economic performance drop drastically.[5] The index lists ten facets of economic freedom, as shown in table 5. In the right hand column is the average score obtained by Latin America in each category.

---

3 Marc Miles, Edwin J. Feulner, Mary Anastasia O'Grady, Ana Isabel Eiras, and Aaron Schavey, *2004 Index of Economic Freedom*, The Heritage Foundation and *The Wall Street Journal*, 2004.

4 "What Is Economic Freedom?" http://www.heritage.org/Index/.

5 "2004 Index of Economic Freedom Shows Quick Economic Benefits for Those Countries That Open Their Economies," *Financial News*, Press Release, January 8, 2004, http://www.thefreelibrary.com/2004+%27Index+of+Economic+Freedom%27+Shows+Quick+Economic+Benefits+for...-a0111994791.

Table 3
Ten Factors of Economic Freedom

Category	Average Score 2009 Latin America and the Caribbean
Business Freedom: How free entrepreneurs are to start a business (regulation as measured by the Doing Business index).	63.4
Fiscal Freedom: Top income tax rate, tax rate that applies to the average income level, top corporate tax rate, other taxes.	76.6
Trade Freedom: Tariffs and nontariff barriers.	74.1
Government Size: Government expenditures as a percentage of the economy, government ownership of businesses and industries, economic output produced by the government.	72.0
Monetary Freedom: Average inflation rates for various years, price stability.	73.4
Investment Freedom: Restrictions to foreign ownership of business, restrictions on the industries and companies open to foreign investors, restrictions and performance requirements on foreign companies, foreign ownership of land, equal treatment under the law for both foreign and domestic companies, restrictions on the repatriation of earnings, availability of local financing for foreign companies.	50.3
Financial Freedom: Relative openness of the banking and financial system services	48.6
Labor Freedom: Wage and hour restrictions on labor, rigidities in the labor market.	60.5

Property Rights: Freedom from government influence over the judicial system, commercial code defining contracts, sanctioning of foreign arbitration of contract disputes, government expropriation of property, corruption within the judiciary, delays in receiving judicial decisions, legally granted and protected private property.	43.4
Freedom from Corruption: Smuggling, piracy of intellectual property in the black market, agricultural production supplied on the black market, manufacturing supplied on the black market, services supplied on the black market, transportation supplied on the black market, labor supplied on the black market.	38.6

Source: Terry Miller and Kim R. Holmes, *2009 Index of Economic Freedom*. (USA: The Heritage Foundation and *The Wall Street Journal*, 2009). The document is downloadable in full at www.heritage.org.

Of the countries measured in Latin America and the Caribbean in the 2011 edition of the index, Chile is the best performer with a score of 77.4 (slightly lower than in previous years), and Cuba is the worst, with 27.7 points. Only three countries in the region qualify as mostly free in 2011: Chile, St. Lucia, and Uruguay. Barbados and The Bahamas have been on this short list in previous years. Brazil, the rising star, ranks 21 in the region and 113 worldwide. The most improved countries in the region are Colombia (+2.5) and Belize (+2.3).[6]

Most Latin American countries have fragile property rights regimes and struggle against corruption. Both are related to rule of law institutions. A sad showing in these areas neutralizes the

6 2009 index, chapter 5, http://www.heritage.org/Index/Explore.aspx; see also 2011 chapter 3, same website. Miller and Holmes also edit the 2011 index.

gains made in other respects, such as trade liberalization. What is more, those countries in which property rights are secure are also the freest countries.

The Institutional Quality Index (IQI) confirms the picture that emerges from the freedom index. This study is a composite of eight indexes, half of which are concerned with political freedom and half with economic freedom. On the political side, the IQI feeds from two World Bank measures: the rule of law index and governance and accountability rankings. It also incorporates the corruption perception index conducted by Transparency International, and Freedom House's freedom of press index. The economic side of the equation is a composite of Doing Business, the World Economic Forum's Global Competitiveness measure, and both the Fraser Institute and the *Wall Street Journal*/Heritage Foundation indexes of economic freedom.[7]

Although some of the rankings vary slightly, the worst and best performers retain their places: Chile, The Bahamas, Saint Lucia, and Barbados top the IQI list, which incidentally includes Canada (1) and the United States (2). Chile was first in Latin America in 2007 and 2008, but the next year fell behind the Caribbean nations mentioned above. The worst performers in both studies are Cuba, Venezuela, and Haiti. These countries have occupied the last places in the IQI ranking for several consecutive years.

[7] For the Institutional Quality Index of 2008, see http://www.policynetwork.net/es/development/publication/es/2008-institutional-quality-index spanish and 2009, see http://www.policynetwork.net/node/33.

Table 4
Economic Freedom and Institutional Quality Compared
Latin America and the Caribbean Rankings

Country	Economic Freedom 2011		IQI 2009	
	World Rank	Region Rank	World Rank	Region Rank
Chile	11	1	24	4
Saint Lucia	26	2	23	3
Uruguay	33	3	60	14
El Salvador	39	4	77	19
Peru	41	5	83	21
Barbados	42	6	39	9
Colombia	45	7	97	22
The Bahamas	46	8	29	6
Mexico	48	9	79	20
Costa Rica	49	10	52	12
St. Vincent and Grenadines	50	11	28	5
Trinidad and Tobago	52	12	67	16
Jamaica	58	13	66	15
Panama	59	14	68	17
Belize	71	15	76	18
Dominica	72	16	44	10
Paraguay	77	17	136	32
Guatemala	79	18	109	27
Dominican Republic	90	19	102	25
Nicaragua	98	20	116	29
Honduras	99	21	106	26
Brazil	113	22	98	23

Suriname	129	23	101	24
Haiti	133	24	164	35
Argentina	138	25	114	28
Bolivia	147	26	133	31
Guyana	151	27	130	30
Ecuador	158	28	144	33
Venezuela	175	29	174	36
Cuba	177	30	162	34
St. Kitts and Nevis	Not Measured	Not Measured	32	7
Puerto Rico	N/M	N/M	34	8
Antigua and Barbuda	N/M	N/M	47	11
Granada	N/M	N/M	58	13

Sources: *The Wall Street Journal* and The Heritage Foundation 2011; Institutional Quality Index 2009.

Once again, we see how countries that have problems with the rule of law are also the countries that are more corrupt and least competitive. These are the least free.

The rule of law is a set of social institutions or "man-made rules which constrain possibly arbitrary and opportunistic behavior in human interactions."[8] The World Justice Project is a relatively young organization that heralds a "worldwide rule of law deficit." It is developing a Rule of Law Index similar to the others here reviewed. The project has managed to define four characteristics present in systems with rule of law. There ought to be accountability under the law for government and all public servants. Laws ought to be "clear, publicized, stable and fair"

[8] Wolfgang Kasper and Manfred Streit, *Institutional Economics: Social Order and Public Policy* (Cheltenham, UK: Edward Elgar, 1998), 28.

and they should uphold the basic personal right to security and property. Laws ought to be enacted and administered through "accessible, fair and efficient" processes. Fourthly, those who adjudicate justice must act independently. They must be ethical and competent and a reflection of their community makeup. To this end, administrators of justice must receive sufficient funds and be "sufficient in number."[9]

The rule of law serves to frame and uphold property rights, which the indexes show are crucial to achieving greater economic growth. Enrique Ghersi and Hernando De Soto, among others, have shown how a stable regime of property rights is linked to poverty reduction and to the expansion of entrepreneurialism. Summarizing these authors' work, O'Driscoll and Hoskin write: "Once an extralegal entrepreneur becomes legal and can title his assets, the whole world of credit opens up to him."[10] It has been estimated that the poor hold at least $9.3 trillion in "dead capital," or untitled assets; if their property rights were recognized and securely enforced, these informal owners would not only be better off, but they would also be able to stand up to corruption.[11]

---

[9] The World Justice Project, http://www.worldjusticeproject.org.

[10] Gerald P. O'Driscoll and Lee Hoskins, "Property Rights: The Key to Economic Development," *Policy Analysis*, August 7, 2003, 12.

[11] The property-rights interest in the writings of Enrique Ghersi and Hernando De Soto echoes the work of modern-day economists concerned with institutions and property rights; namely, Armen Alchian, Ronald Coase, and Harold Demsetz. Coase, for instance, not only defined property rights but also emphasized that governments are not entirely responsible for defining and protecting said rights; this is also achieved through custom and tradition, as well as contracts and other voluntary forms of exchange. Enrique Ghersi and Hernando De Soto first published *The Other Path* in 1986. In this book, they document informal markets in Peru. De Soto has since worked around the world to help governments wishing to recognize and guarantee property entitlements, and published *The Mystery of Capital: Why Capitalism Triumphs in the West and Fails Everywhere Else* (New York: Basic Books, 2000). Enrique Ghersi, a

In economist Peter Boettke's words:

> When property rights are so embedded in an environment where they "stick," the path to property leads to the path to prosperity in short order. Property rights provide the foundation for the market economy. Without private property rights there would be no exchange, and without exchange there would be no prices, and without prices there would be no rational accounting based on profit and loss statements. The three Ps of property, prices and profit/loss provide within a dynamic economy the three Is of incentives, information and innovation.[12]

The three Ps and the three Is are complemented by the three Ds that describe the nature of properly functioning property rights. Property should be defined, defensible, and divestible. We have already mentioned the importance of clearly defining rights to all forms of property. A property owner must be able to defend his rights against abuse by government or a third party. In other words, the legal and judicial systems in place must enable him to exercise his right exclusively. Finally, an owner must be able to divest or transfer his property by bequeathing, renting, selling, or otherwise disposing of it. Transferability guarantees that scarce resources will pass into the hands of people who most value the resources at the time, assuring its productive employment.[13]

The entrepreneur, and more extensively, any productive member of society, responds to the incentives created by the property

---

lawyer, has since fleshed out ideas on legal and judicial institutions and their roles in clarifying and upholding property rights.

[12] Peter Boettke, foreword to *Paths to Property*, ed. Boudreaux and Aligica, 12.

[13] For more on the three Ds of property rights, refer to Richard Stroup, *Eco-nomics* (Washington, D.C.: Cato Institute, 2003). Two additional helpful sources are Henri Lepage, *Porqué la propiedad* (Madrid: Instituto de Estudios Económicos, 1986); and Thomas Bethell, *The Noblest Triumph* (New York: St. Martin's Griffin, 1998).

rights regime and the rule of law infrastructure in each country. Yet, it is also said that these people possess *human capital*, a term popularized by the 1992 Nobel Prize winner in economics, Gary Becker. Workers gain skills and knowledge through education and experience, and this enables them to produce economic value. This accumulation of knowledge and experience is human capital.

Ever since Becker first triggered interest in human capital in 1964, policy makers have sought to foster or stimulate its formation, mainly through state-run education models. Asia's economic stars, it is said, heavily invested in education, and this is the reason for their success. Latin America, on the other hand, is lagging behind the world in terms of quality and coverage. Becker's work, however, in no way implies that all formal education and only formal education contributes to human capital. In low-income countries, publicly provided education services can be so deficient as to become irrelevant to the formation of human capital. Moreover, knowledge acquired outside the classroom, especially on-the-job-training, is valued human capital.

Sometimes human capital is tied to the concept of social capital, which reflects an interest in how interrelations affect personal well-being and economic growth. Families are both institutions and a form of social capital. Research demonstrates that family structure affects human capital. A child living in a two-parent home that furnishes her with a secure, stable, and loving environment not only tends to learn more in the customary sense of conventional school subjects, but she also tends to acquire those "life skills" that are arguably more important for successful integration into the productive economy: a sense of responsibility, moral integrity and honesty, reliability and consistency as a worker, and the capacity to interact positively with others. As Becker notes, "learning begets learning"; these children possess an advantage over those who hail from less stable home environments. Nonintact households affect children in various ways: more school dropouts and worse grades, more delinquency in minors, more drug use, more suicidal tendencies, and so on. Research also shows a dramatic advantage in terms of levels of wealth for intact households as compared to other family structures. In other words, the age-old institution of the intact family contributes to the social and economic wellbeing of its members, as well as to economic growth.[14]

In *How the West Grew Rich*, Nathan Rosenberg and L. E. Birdzell Jr. explain how it is that entrepreneurship and the "right" institutions can provoke economic growth. They do so by reviewing the economic history of the West. These authors demonstrate that growth came from a double decentralization both in enterprises and in innovation. Western economies have been more or less open throughout history. That is to say that people, families, firms, and other voluntary associations have been able to offer and purchase various goods and services. In a free market, people are enterprising; they make decisions and take risks without being coerced. If the product supplied is welcome by potential customers, then investors harvest a profit. Otherwise they lose. The market is dynamic and flexible. Millions of actors make their own decisions without being influenced or directed by a central planner. Authority, power, and control are distributed among thousands upon thousands of people.

Decentralized entrepreneurship is intimately linked to decentralized innovation. Only when we are free to choose do we create, innovate, explore, and discover.[15] The power to start innovation projects and to find a practical application for new technologies is again distributed widely among all members of society. As

---

[14] Gary S. Becker, *El capital humano, un análisis teórico y empírico referido fundamentalmente a la educación* (Madrid, Alianza Editorial, 1975; first pub. in English in 1964). For a study on the Guatemalan family and economic growth, see Maria Sophia Aguirre, *Determinantes del Crecimiento Económico, Población y Familia: El Caso Guatemala* (Guatemala: Familia Desarrollo y Población [FADEP], 2007).

[15] Israel Kirzner has written extensively on the role of the entrepreneur and the discovery process. See for instance *Competition and Entrepreneurship* (Chicago: University of Chicago Press, 1978).

Birdzell and Rosenberg put it: "For enterprises to realize the rewards and suffer the penalties that go with the selection of programs of innovation, they have to be responsible for selecting their markets, determining the prices at which they will buy and sell and the wages at which they will hire, hiring and dismissing their employees, and investing capital."[16]

What role should governments play in a free market environment? As has been seen, Catholic social teaching preserves for government the right and responsibility to intervene in the economy when necessary for the common good. The evidence from countless nations and centuries of development (and lack thereof), a small part of which we have presented above, leads to the conclusion that government intervention should be minimal. In general, governments should refrain from participating directly in markets by controlling or favoring individual industries, businesses, or groups of businesses. Governments should also be careful not to regulate business excessively, which, despite good intentions, leads to the unintended consequences of stifling business activity, inhibiting job growth, and preventing innovation. The Church recognizes the critical role of the market, which is easily impinged on by state action:

> *A truly competitive market is an effective instrument for attaining important objectives of justice*: moderating the excessive profits of individual businesses, responding to consumers' demands, bringing about a more efficient use and conservation of resources, rewarding entrepreneurship and innovation, making information available so that it is really possible to compare and purchase products in an atmosphere of healthy competition. (CSD, no. 347)

Governments should concentrate on providing security and effective judicial services. Pope Benedict XVI urges that the proper

---

16 Nathan Rosenberg and L. E. Birdzell, *How the West Grew Rich* (New York: Basic Books, 1986), 267.

"State of law," understood as "a system of public order and effective imprisonment that respects human rights, truly democratic institutions" must be strengthened. He presents a decentralized vision where each level of authority discharges its own proper duties:

> The State does not need to have identical characteristics everywhere: the support aimed at strengthening weak constitutional systems can easily be accompanied by the development of other political players, of a cultural, social, territorial or religious nature, alongside the State. The articulation of political authority at the local, national and international levels is one of the best ways of giving direction to the process of economic globalization. (CV, no. 41)

Rosenberg and Nathan suggest that government activism can reach a point where it is no longer politically beneficial, precisely because it limits economic growth. In other words, some state projects such as public schools and highways can enhance growth, but they mischievously add: "It is entirely possible that an exaggerated belief in the capacity of government to enhance economic welfare has created more havoc in the political sphere than in the economic."[17] The danger is that government involvement in economic projects can easily become a source of corruption, when projects are undertaken and firms contracted on political rather than economic grounds. The key is identifying this turning point from legitimate government involvement to excessive government interference and staying on the right side of the imaginary border.

[17] Rosenberg and Birdzell, *How the West Grew Rich*, 308

V Lesson Learned, Reform Deferred, and the Return of Populism

Latin Americans ought to give freedom a trial run. Less-developed countries cannot mimic nor reproduce the Western experience for historic, cultural, and political reasons. Herein lies the dilemma. Even though Latin American governments are ever more conscious of what it is they ought to do, the incentive structure in politics is such that government officials resist reforming in the "correct" direction. If a reform is perceived as imposing short-term costs on society, and therefore harming the public servant's political popularity, it is less appealing. Business elites, accustomed to protectionism and to rent-seeking behaviors, reject reforms because it is easier or cheaper to lobby governments than to compete in free markets. Greater economic growth through free markets will make us all better off in the future, but the decision to implement liberalization policies will be based on the concentrated benefits and low costs awarded by the status quo to individual officers and certain sectors of society.

Abrupt shifts in power, such as the 1973 overthrow of President Salvador Allende in Chile and perhaps the current crisis, can provide unique opportunities for comprehensive structural reform. One would hope that freer economies would emerge within the democratic framework, not in conjunction with authoritarianism, as was the case in Chile. There is no deterministic link between free markets and repressive governments.

The power to coerce can lead to situations of abuse and to human rights violations, where governments, however well intentioned, can impose undesired costs on the very citizens they are supposed to serve. The solution is not more government, then, but rule of law and constitutional constraints: clear limits on arbitrary political power, separation of powers, fragmentation of power into decentralized entities, and other checks and balances. Barring the Alberdi constitution in Argentina[1] and the more recent attempts to "modernize" and downsize public administration to reduce it to a subsidiary role in a few countries, this "preventive" attitude toward government has been absent from the Latin American political landscape.

The perception that Latin America has oscillated from interventionism to liberalization and back again is mistaken. It would be foolish to deny that some modest efforts have been made to convert the mercantilist state system into a state that is more consistent with the rule of law. The Chile experiment and more recent liberalization attempts sought to reduce the size and scope of government action in Latin America. Yet, even the most adventurous liberalization strategies have tended to award governments a leading role in designing, guiding, and regulating economies. Latin Americans have never really given freedom a chance.

After sifting through annual data sets, Economic Freedom Index editors Miller and Holmes recommend long-term implementation of policies that promote economic freedom in order to achieve development; going into reverse merely postpones prosperity. In Latin America, however, they see erosion in economic freedom prompted by a return of populist policies.

Populism is associated with Latin American political history. Some say this is the region of the world most influenced

[1] Juan Batista Alberdi's proposed constitution was adopted by Argentina in 1853. It is one of the longest lasting constitutions in Latin America, as it did not undergo substantial reform until 1957.

by populism, as a variety of left and right leaning governments have "made political promises to the citizenry with the illusion of solving its problems through magic."[2]

Populism in Latin America tends to consist of a strange cocktail of nationalism, socialism, and demagoguery. It is accompanied by incendiary speeches that pit poor against rich, as well as the local masses against "foreign imperialism" and "economic dominance" exerted by developed countries. Iconic populist leaders of the twentieth century include Juan Domingo Perón in Argentina and Getulio Vargas in Brazil. Both had military backgrounds and were not necessarily advocates of democratic practices. They both used their personal charisma to mobilize the masses. They used an antipolitical discourse that weakened both the existing administrative structures and the legal limits to power. The charismatic leader became the paternal mediator on behalf of the "downtrodden" and formerly disenfranchised people.[3] Today, this style of politics tends to be associated with figures such as Venezuela's Hugo Chávez and the president of Bolivia, Evo Morales.

---

2 Cristián Larroulet and Barbara Horzella, "Populismo en América Latina: Paradigma y Antítesis en los casos de Venezuela y Chile," *Las Frágiles Democracias Latinoamericanas* (Buenos Aires: CADAL/Atlas Foundation, 2008), 105.

3 Some publications dealing with populism and neopopulism in Latin America include: Enrique Krauze, "Decálogo del populismo iberoamericano," *El País*, October 14, 2005, http://www.elpais.com/articulo/opinion/Decalogo/populismo/iberoamericano/elpporopi/20051014elpepiopi_7/Tes; Julio A. Cirino, "Latin America 'Populism for the XXI Century': Walking Forward—Looking Backward," http://www.gwu.edu/~clai/recent_events/2006/060921-NeoPopulism_Cirino_Paper.pdf; Alan Knight, "Populism and Neo-Populism in Latin America, Especially Mexico," *Journal of Latin American Studies* 30, no. 2 (May 1998): 223–48; Ernesto Lucena, *Latin American Tendency Towards Presidential Re-election Has Taken Its Toll on Colombia*, Universidad Sergio Arboleda School of Law, Colombia, http://www.ialsnet.org/meetings/constit/papers/LucenaErnesto(Colombia).pdf.

Nonetheless, the Latin-American brand of populism is not an ideology but rather an opportunistic form or style of governing that frequently cultivates ideological ambiguities. Neo-populist leaders have proven to be more adept than traditional populists in the use of democratic processes, reforming legal instruments including constitutions to expand their power, handling macro-economic policies, using the mass media, and establishing regional organizations to coordinate efforts.

Economic measures include the expropriation of property, regulation, tax hikes, greater state participation in the economy, and investment in vote-fetching social programs. For instance, during his first eleven years in power, Venezuelan president Hugo Chávez confiscated a total of 1,750 private businesses, large and small, in agriculture, petroleum, commerce, and other sectors, according to Fernando Morgado, president of the National Council for Commerce and Services (Consecomercio).[4] In past decades, economic policies also involved reckless monetary and inflationary policies; now leaders are more cautious regarding inflation but still have tended to run up the fiscal deficit.[5]

Populism brings economic malaise. Once the demagogic clouds dissipate, the average citizen has not been liberated from oppressive corporate elites or from corruption. New political elites are created, who are even more corrupt and who maintain policies that prolong poverty. By this time, the rule of law has been heavily eroded, property rights are shattered, and entrepreneurship has been stifled, thus making recovery an uphill battle.

The long-lasting effects of populism in the region are worrisome for three reasons. First, populist leaders have thus far had

---

4 "Chávez ha expropiado más de 1,700 empresas durante su gestión," *Fortunaweb*, October 12, 2010, http://fortunaweb.com.ar/chavez-ya-expropio-mas-de-1-700-empresas-durante-su-gestion/. Hugo Chávez assumed office in 1999.

5 Sebastian Edward, *Populismo o mercados, el dilema de América Latina* (Bogotá: Norma, 2009).

the resources to promote aggressive foreign policy agendas that include influencing electoral processes as well as diplomatic and economic policies in other countries. Second, populism entrenches corruption in political and social spheres and erodes the rule of law and democratic forms of government. Corrupt environments are fertile ground for drug trafficking organizations, which are best described as international corporations. These have been associated with rising crime numbers and gang-related violence in the region. Third and last, the mainstream plea for "more government" that arose as a seemingly logical petition from the collapse of the world financial markets is music to the populists' ears. More government is not necessarily a good thing, much less in countries where populism has taken hold of the political decision making processes.

As stated at the outset, one unintended consequence of recommending greater government intervention in the economy, with the manifestly benign intention of avoiding future crises, is that such intervention will be harmful in countries with frail institutional arrangements. We face a new reality. The main threats to the democratic system do not come from violent overthrows or foreign invasions but from within. "What we see today in Latin America ... is the extreme fragility that the democratic regimes in the region possess; their weakness in the face of demagoguery and populism, when these decide to use the existing liberties to capture power and destroy the institutions and the values on which the democratic liberal system is based."[6]

---

6 Carlos Sabino, "Democracia," unpublished paper, 2010.

VI Conclusion

The world financial crisis had some negative impact on Latin American economies. This affects all inhabitants of the region and the families of émigrés, including those who live in poverty and extreme poverty.

The crisis also taught us that economists and other social scientists are not gods: Their limited tools are unable to predict the future. What will happen within a very complex system such as global society, which encompasses global markets and political processes at various levels, defies prediction.

Two conflicting solutions ensue from this realization. I favor the one that rejects the fatal arrogance of the planner. Not only should we accept in humility the consequences of the myriads of interactions of free men and women, we should be awestruck by them. For this organic exchange to bring prosperity, a set of general, abstract, and legitimate rules and their respective enforcement mechanisms must be in place—not to bring forth predictable results but to guarantee basic human rights. The contrary approach is to blame this marvelous interaction for the global collapse and to attempt to "save" the market through government intervention. It is a prevalent view—although the challenge of planning for a global society is daunting and perhaps utopian.

Solid institutions of entrepreneurship, effective formation of human capital, robust property rights, and rule of law could greatly contribute to raising the living standards of Latin America and eradicating poverty in the region. In fact, a peaceful transition from development-adverse institutions to growth-oriented institutions would accomplish more than the public policy agenda and the donations peddled by international organizations and the governments of developed nations.

Like wealth itself, these institutions are a *means*, not an end. There ought to be a multitude of ends—as many as there are human beings. The institutional means serve the same purpose as roads: They enable rule-abiding drivers to reach their destination but do not dictate its location. Markets also act like roads, enabling people to pursue their own dreams, to innovate, and to serve each other.

If, as *Caritas in Veritate* affirms, progress is a personal vocation (no. 11), then social order should be such that each free and responsible citizen can follow a unique calling. This calling is made whole by our voluntary embrace of God's mandate to love one another as He loves us. We must undertake this journey with great optimism, Pope Benedict reminds us, for globalization, technological advances, and other novelties of our time are but opportunities. If globalization is an opportunity, then so, too, can the financial crisis be an opportunity. It can be a catalyst for institutional reform. We are architects, not victims, of the future.

References

Church Documents, with Abbreviations

The following documents are available online at www.vatican.va.

John Paul II, *Centesimus Annus* (1991), CA.

Catechism of the Catholic Church (1994), CCC.

Pontifical Council for Justice and Peace, *Compendium of the Social Doctrine of the Church* (1995), CSD.

Benedict XVI, *Caritas in Veritate* (2009), CV.

Benedict XVI, *Deus Caritas Est* (2005), DCE.

Second Vatican Council, *Gaudium et Spes* (1965), GS.

John XXIII, *Mater et Magistra* (1961), MM.

Leo XIII, *Rerum Novarum* (1891), RN.

John Paul II, *Sollicitudo Rei Socialis* (1987), SRS.

Books and Articles

Aguirre, Maria Sophia. *Determinantes del Crecimiento Económico, Población y Familia: El Caso Guatemala*. Guatemala: Familia Desarrollo y Población (FADEP), 2007.

Ayau, Manuel. "La Distribución de la Riqueza." In *El Proceso Económico*. Mexico: Diana, 1995.

———. *Not a Zero-Sum Game*. Guatemala: Universidad Francisco Marroquin, 2007.

Bárcena, Alicia. "Latin America and the Caribbean: Challenges and Opportunities in a Time of Crisis" (September 11, 2009). http://www.slideshare.net/Cepal/latin-america-and-the-caribbean-challenges-and-opportunities-in-a-time-of-crisis.

Bauer, P. T. "Disregard of Reality." *The Cato Journal* 7 (Spring/Summer 1987): 29–42.

———. *From Subsistence to Exchange and Other Essays*. Princeton, N.J.: Princeton University Press, 2000.

———. *The Rubber Industry*. London: Longmans Green and Co., 1948.

Becker, Gary S. *El capital humano, un análisis teórico y empírico referido fundamentalmente a la educación*. Madrid: Alianza Editorial, 1975 (Chicago: University of Chicago Press, 1964).

Bethell, Thomas. *The Noblest Triumph*. New York: St. Martin's Griffin, 1998.

Bodreaux, Karl, and Paul Dragos Aligica. *Paths to Property: Approaches to Institutional Change in International Development*. London: Institute of Economic Affairs, 2007.

Bolt, John. "Christian Obligations: 'The Poor You Will Always Have with You.'" *Journal of Markets & Morality* 7 (Fall 2004): 467–93.

De Soto, Hernando, and Enrique Ghersi. *El Otro Sendero*. Perú: Editorial El Barranco, 1986.

Delgado Aguilera, Rodrigo, et al. *From Steady Growth to Sudden Crisis: How Latin America and the Caribbean Are Coping with the Global Recession*. International Economics Working Paper: IEP WP 09/01. London: Chatham House (May 2009). http://www.chathamhouse.org.uk/publications/papers/view/-/id/744/.

Dent, Harry. http://www.hsdent.com.

Doing Business 2011: Making a Difference for Entrepreneurs. Washington, D.C.: The International Bank for Reconstruction and Development/

The World Bank, 2010. http://www.doingbusiness.org/~/media/fpdkm/doing%20business/documents/annual-reports/english/db11-fullreport.pdf.

Dorn, James A. "P. T. Bauer's Liberal Market Vision." *Ideas on Liberty* 50 (October 2000). http://www.thefreemanonline.org/featured/p-t-bauers-market-liberal-vision/.

Easterly, William. *The Elusive Quest for Growth: Economists' Adventures and Misadventures in the Tropics.* Cambridge: MIT Press, 2002.

Edward, Sebastian. *Populismo o Mercados, El Dilema de América Latina.* Bogotá: Norma, 2009.

Fajnzylber, Pablo, and Humberto López. "El impacto de las remesas en el desarrollo de América Latina." http://www.remesasydesarrollo.org/estadisticas/remittances-and-development-lessons-from-latin-america/.

"Foreign Direct Investment in Latin America and the Caribbean." United Nations Economic Commission for Latin American and the Caribbean (ECLAC) Briefing Paper (May 2010). http://www.eclac.org/cgi-bin/getProd.asp?xml=/publicaciones/xml/2/39422/P39422.xml&xsl=/ddpe/tpl-i/p9f.xsl&base=/prensa/tpl-i/top-bottom.xsl.

"Fiscal Policy in Times of Crisis: Volatility, Social Cohesion and the Political Economy of Reform." Forum of the European Union, Latin America, and the Caribbean. Montevideo, Uruguay (May 19–20, 2009). http://ec.europa.eu/external_relations/lac/fiscalforum/2009_05_prog_es.pdf.

"From Financial Crisis to Rural Social Crisis in Latin America," Summary Report on International Fund for Agricultural Development (IFAD) Conference, Rome (April 23–24, 2009). http://www.ifad.org/media/press/2009/21.htm.

Fujita, Masataka. "Implications of the Financial and Economic Crisis on FDI: An Updated Assessment." Investment Trends and Data Section, *UNCTAD* (April 17, 2009). http://nku.com.cn/UploadFile/200941402013964.pdf.

"Government Support for Financial Assets and Liabilities Announced in 2008 and Soon Thereafter." FDIC Supervisory Insights (Summer 2009). http://www.fdic.gov/regulations/examinations/supervisory/insights/sisum09/si_sum09.pdf.

Gutierrez, Miguel. "Perspectivas Económicas 2010 para Guatemala y el Mundo, ¿Fin de la Crisis o Espejismos?" Unpublished Paper. Social and Economic Research Center (CEES), Guatemala (November 17, 2009).

2011 Index of Economic Freedom. Various authors and years. The Heritage Foundation and *The Wall Street Journal*. http://www.heritage.org/Index/.

Krause, Martin. Institutional Quality Index 2008. http://www.policynetwork.net/es/development/publication/es/2008-institutional-quality-index-spanish.

Kasper, Wolfgang, and Manfred Streit. *Institutional Economics: Social Order and Public Policy*. Cheltenham, United Kingdom: Edward Elgar, 1998.

Kirzner, Israel. *Competition and Entrepreneurship*. Chicago: University of Chicago Press, 1978.

Larroulet, Cristián, and Barbara Horzella. "Populismo en América Latina: Paradigma y Antítesis en los casos de Venezuela y Chile." In *Las Frágiles Democracias Latinoamericanas*. Buenos Aires: CADAL/Atlas Foundation, 2008.

Lastrero, Rodrigo. "El aumento de la pobreza en América Latina, la secuela más ingrata de la crisis" (August 27, 2009). http://www.degerencia.com/noticia/29341/el-aumento-de-la-pobreza-en-america-latina-la-secuela-mas-ingrata-de-la-crisis.

———. "La Obreza Reina en el Mundo Hispano." *Univisión* (September 28, 2005). http://www.univision.com/content/content.jhtml?cid=674281.

"Latin America Economic Outlook 2011: How Middle-Class Is Latin America?" OECD Development Center, 2010. http://www.latameconomy.org/fileadmin/uploads/laeo/Documents/E-book_LEo2011-EN_entier.pdf.

Leeson, Peter. "Two Cheers for Capitalism?" www.peterleeson.com/Two_Cheers_for_Capitalism.pdf.

Lepage, Henri. *Porqué la Propiedad.* Madrid: Instituto de Estudios Económicos, 1986.

López, J. Humberto, and Luis Servén. "Too Poor to Grow." World Bank Working Paper No. 5012 (August 2009).

McCoy, Terry, and Timothy McLendon. *2009 Latin America Business Environment Report*, University of Florida, October, 2009. Available at http://www.docs.google.com.

Montecarlo, Victor. "Disminuye Pobreza en el Mundo." *International Business Times* (September 9, 2008). http://www.ibtimes.com.mx.

"More or Less Equal?" *The Economist* (March 11, 2004). http://www.economist.com.

Mueller, Antony P. "Financial Cycles, Business Activity, and the Stock Market." *Quarterly Journal of Austrian Economics* 4 (Spring 2001). http://mises.org/journals/qjae/pdf/qjae4_1_1.pdf.

Noriega, Roger F. "Latin America and the Economic Crisis: Going It Alone." *Latin American Outlook.* American Enterprise Institute (June 2009). http://www.aei.org.

O'Driscoll, Gerald P., and Lee Hoskins. "Property Rights: The Key to Economic Development." *Policy Analysis* (August 7, 2003).

Powell, Benjamin, ed. *Making Poor Nations Rich: Entrepreneurship and the Process of Economic Development.* Stanford, Calif.: Stanford University Press, 2007.

"BID: Remesas a América Latina caerán 11% en 2009." *Dinero.com* (August 12, 2009).

"Remittances to Latin America and the Caribbean Slower, IADB Fund Says" (March 11, 2008). http://www.iadb.org/news/detail.cfm?language=EN&artid=4459&id=4459.

Rosenberg, Nathan, and L. E. Birdzell. *How the West Grew Rich.* New York: Basic Books, 1986.

Rule of Law Index, as conceptualized by the World Justice Project, www.worldjusticeproject.org.

Sabino, Carlos. "Mitos Sobre la Pobreza." http://paginas.ufm.edu/sabino/ingles/book/mitos_pobreza.pdf.

Sala-i-Martin, Xavier. "Global Inequality Fades as the Global Economy Grows." In *2007 Index of Economic Freedom: The Link Between Economic Opportunity and Prosperity*. Edited by Tim Kane, Kim R. Holmes, and Mary Anastasia O'Grady. Washington, D.C.: The Heritage Foundation and *The Wall Street Journal*, 2007.

Schiff, Peter. http://www.moneyweek.com/news-and-charts/peter-schiff-free-marketeer-who-predicted-the-crisis-45136.aspx.

Stroup, Richard. *Eco-nomics*. Washington, D.C.: Cato Institute, 2003.

Suárez Vélez, Jorge. "Crisis Financiera en el Mundo y su Efecto para Latinoamérica." Twelfth Conference on Financial Supervision sponsored by the Banks Superintendence (SIB). Guatemala (August 27, 2009).

UNCTAD's *World Investment Report 2005: Transnational Corporations and the Internationalization of R&D*. http://www.unctad.org/Templates/WebFlyer.asp?intItemID=3489&lang=1.

Vargas Llosa, Alvaro. *Lessons from the Poor: Triumph of the Entrepreneurial Spirit*. Oakland, Calif.: The Independent Institute, 2008.

Woods, Thomas E. Jr. *Meltdown: A Free-Market Look at Why the Stock Market Collapsed, the Economy Tanked, and Government Bailouts Will Make Things Worse*. Washington, D.C.: Regnery Publishing, 2009.

Yunus, Muhammad. "How Could the World Change Through Micro-credit." Lecture at Universidad Francisco Marroquín, Guatemala (December 10, 2007).

About the Author

Carroll Ríos de Rodríguez teaches Public Choice theory and development economics at Francisco Marroquín University in Guatemala, where, as of July 2010, she also serves as president of the Board of Trustees. She serves on the Boards of Directors of the Economics and Social Research Center (CEES) and of the Family, Development and Population Association (FADEP), and is a member of the Mont Pelerin Society. Rodríguez writes a weekly column for the Guatemalan daily *Siglo Veintiuno*, and her articles have been published by Friedrich Naumann Foundation's *Perfiles Liberales*, Cato Institute's *Regulation* magazine, and *The Wall Street Journal*, among others. She obtained a bachelor of arts degree from Dartmouth College and a master of arts degree in Latin American Studies from Georgetown University.